THE BOGEYMAN

monster
Chronicles

THE BOGEYMAN

STEPHEN KRENSKY

Lerner Publications Company · Minneapolis

Lerner Publications Company
A division of Lerner Publishing Group, Inc.
241 First Avenue North
Minneapolis, MN 55401 U.S.A.

Website address: www.lernerbooks.com

Library of Congress Cataloging-in-Publication Data

Krensky, Stephen.
    The bogeyman / by Stephen Krensky.
        p.   cm. — (Monster chronicles)
    Includes bibliographical references and index.
    ISBN-13: 978-0-8225-6760-8 (lib. bdg. : alk. paper)
        1. Monsters—Europe. 2. Monsters—United States. I. Title.
    GR135.K74 2008
    398'.45—dc22   2006101867

Manufactured in the United States of America
1 2 3 4 5 6 - JR - 13 12 11 10 09 08

TABLE OF CONTENTS

1 Things That Go Bump in the Night

When it comes to monsters, the bogeyman is special. Most monsters have physical limitations. They look a certain way—with hair, teeth, and horns in predictable places. They have a fixed shape and size. They have specific strengths and weaknesses. Bogeymen are not so limited. Sometimes they are said to take human form. Other times they look like animals or strange monsters. The word *bogeyman* covers a lot of ground. It is a catchall name for a scary creature that doesn't fit into any neat and tidy category.

In some ways, it is easiest to define a bogeyman by explaining what he is *not*. Vampires are not bogeymen. Neither are werewolves, goblins, ghosts, or zombies. Frankenstein's monster is not a bogeyman (although he may be just as frightening to the villagers who live nearby). A mummy who comes back from the dead might be scary and dangerous. But that doesn't make him a bogeyman.

Nobody ever talks about a good bogeyman, a kind bogeyman, or

even a misunderstood bogeyman. Unlike sprites, bogeymen do more than make mischief. They are not content just to turn milk sour or steal eggs from chicken coops. Bogeymen are said to be dangerous. They are always evil, bad, and hateful. No exceptions allowed.

Some monsters like to keep to themselves. They are shy and private, uninterested in human affairs. Bigfoot, for example, does not usually meddle with people. He minds his own business. So although he's a monster, he's not a bogeyman. Unlike Bigfoot, a bogeyman is usually looking for trouble. He is aggressive. Bogeymen do not need to know their victims. They don't need a special reason to attack. They are said to do it because they can.

Bogeymen are never small like fairies or elves. If anything, they are thought to be larger than other monsters. And they don't die easily. No matter what weapons you have, bogeymen are hard to kill. They are often sneaky. They move silently through the underbrush or into people's bedrooms.

All in all, it's safest to stay away from bogeymen. That means avoiding the dark woods and foggy marshes where stories say many bogeymen live. Of course, if a bogeyman lives under your bed or in your closet, he'll be much harder to avoid.

BOGLE, BONEY, AND BUGIS

The history of the word *bogeyman* is not entirely clear. Some experts think it comes from a Scottish word, *bogle,* which means "ghost" or "goblin."

Others trace the word back to Napoleon Bonaparte. This French general and emperor lived from 1769 to 1821. The British called him Boney for short. The British and the French were enemies.

A Good Bogeyman?

It's possible for one person's bogeyman to be
another person's hero. The fictional English outlaw Robin
Hood, for example, was said to steal from the rich and give to
the poor. In Robin Hood stories, he was a savior to the poor. He
gave them money and food. But to the rich, Robin Hood was a
bogeyman of the worst kind. Without warning, he would pop out
of Sherwood Forest to rob them of their money.

The warlike Boney was a scary figure, especially to British children. Over the years, the name Boney might have been changed to "boneyman" and then "bogeyman."

Another explanation comes from Sulawesi, an island in Indonesia in Southeast Asia. Dutch explorers (from the Netherlands) sailed to Sulawesi in the 1600s. They found many different native peoples living on the island. One group was the Bugis. The Bugis made their living by trading with people from other countries. They traveled by sea. However, many Bugis were also pirates—and not particularly nice ones. Throughout the region, people greatly feared these "bugis-men."

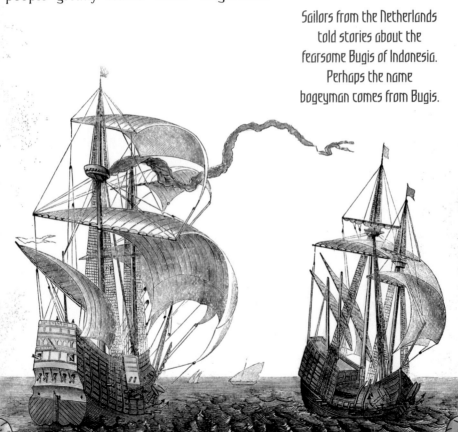

Sailors from the Netherlands told stories about the fearsome Bugis of Indonesia. Perhaps the name bogeyman comes from Bugis.

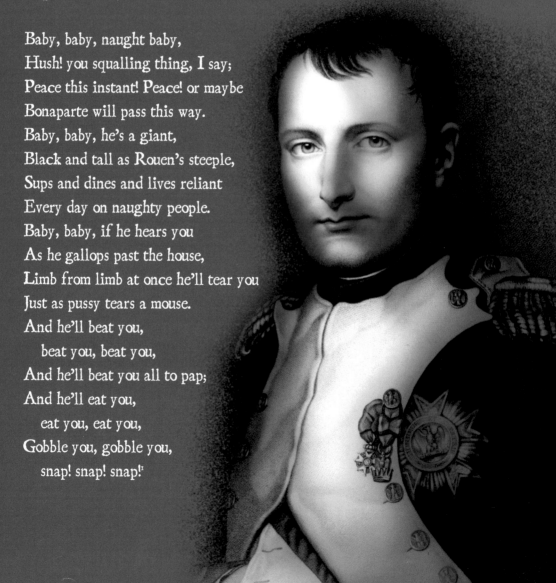

A Scary Nursery Rhyme

This British nursery rhyme warns crying babies to be quiet—or else the bogeyman (French emperor Napoleon Bonaparte, *below*) might come by.

Baby, baby, naught baby,
Hush! you squalling thing, I say;
Peace this instant! Peace! or maybe
Bonaparte will pass this way.
Baby, baby, he's a giant,
Black and tall as Rouen's steeple,
Sups and dines and lives reliant
Every day on naughty people.
Baby, baby, if he hears you
As he gallops past the house,
Limb from limb at once he'll tear you
Just as pussy tears a mouse.
And he'll beat you,
   beat you, beat you,
And he'll beat you all to pap;
And he'll eat you,
   eat you, eat you,
Gobble you, gobble you,
   snap! snap! snap![1]

When Dutch sailors returned home to the Netherlands, they told tales of the fearsome bugis-men. The name might have changed to "bogeymen" and spread to the English language.

Whatever the name's origin, the idea of bogeymen is even older than the name. People probably feared bogeymen as long ago as the Stone Age. That's because dark spaces have always made people nervous. Dark spaces at the back of a Stone Age cave were probably the scariest of all. After all, you never knew what sort of creature might be hiding there.

NAMES AND PLACES

Bogeymen tend to fall into two categories. The first type is an all-purpose scary monster. It is said to wander the countryside looking for victims. It often strikes at night, particularly gloomy nights with no moonlight. The darkness adds to the element of surprise. Bogeymen like that.

The second kind of bogeyman focuses on children. At least, that's what parents want their children to think. For hundreds of years, parents have found it helpful to have a scary creature on hand. Parents who want their children to obey can just mention the creature's name, hoping to frighten the children into listening: "Eat your vegetables or the bogeyman will get you." "Make your bed—because the bogeyman goes after children who don't obey their parents." By the time children figure out that this bogeyman is not real, it's too late—they're already well behaved.

Stories about bogeymen are not limited to one part of the world. They show up in almost every country. In Germany the bogeyman is

known as the Schwarze Mann (the Black Man) because he hides in black or dark places. In Poland he's known as the Bebok. In Romania he's called the Bau-Bau, and in India he's the Bori Baba. Among some Native American groups, the bogeyman is called Wendigo. In Wales, part of Great Britain, he is the Boggart.

Germany's bogey-man, the Schwarze Mann, hides in dark places.

Spain has two kinds of bogeymen. One is El Cuco, a hairy monster that eats children. Another is the Bobalicón. The Bobalicón is a tall monster with a huge head. Fortunately, the Bobalicón is not very smart. His would-be victims stand a fair chance of outwitting him.

Russians facing Baba Yaga may not be so lucky. Unlike most bogeymen, Baba Yaga is a female—a bogeywoman. She is big—as tall as two men and as wide as three. She has fangs. Her eyes can terrify anyone who looks at her. And she can fly. Few people survive a meeting with Baba Yaga because she has the unsettling habit (for them) of eating her victims.

Baba Yaga sometimes flies on an iron kettle. Other times, she flies on a broom-stick, like a witch.

Clearly, bogeymen are not to be treated lightly. Bogeymen are crude, brutal, and mean spirited. They don't have a good sense of humor. This is an appealing combination for them, but not for anyone else.

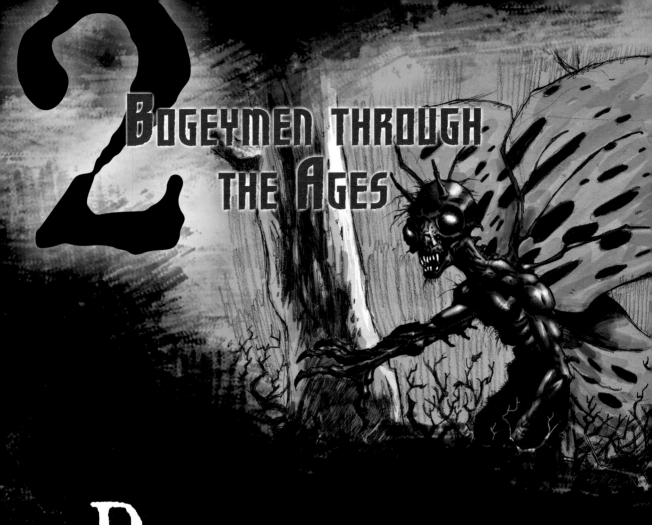

2 Bogeymen Through the Ages

Different bogeymen look different, depending on when and where they show up. Legend has it they often take human form, but are usually much larger than ordinary humans. Some of them have fangs. Some have glowing eyes. Others are covered with hair. No matter what they look like, though, their purpose is always the same—to inspire fear and to perform acts of evil.

FAMOUS BOGEYMEN

Stories of bogeymen (and bogey-women) date to ancient times. One ancient Greek myth describes a bogeywoman named Lamia. She was originally a beautiful woman. She always minded her own business until Zeus, king of the Greek gods, took a fancy to her (as he so often did with beautiful women). But Zeus's wife, Hera, discovered the love affair. Unable to punish Zeus—a more powerful god than she was—Hera took

The British poet John Keats (1795-1821) wrote about Lamia in his poem of the same name. Keats showed Lamia to be both beautiful and tragic.

out her wrath on Lamia. Hera turned Lamia into a monster and killed Lamia's children. Since Hera was a goddess, Lamia was powerless to fight back. So Lamia vented her anger by killing more children. Her victims were innocent and had played no part in her tragedy. That didn't seem to matter to Lamia. By attacking the innocent, Lamia was the perfect bogeywoman.

According to Greek mythology, Lamia has the head and upper body of a woman combined with the lower body of a snake.

Another age-old bogeyman comes from tales in eastern Europe. He is the Golem, a monster from Jewish folktales. Some bogeymen appear out of nowhere. The Golem is different. According to the tales, a rabbi (a Jewish spiritual leader) forms the Golem out of clay. The rabbi brings the monster to life by placing a magical tablet under his tongue. The Golem may look like a real person, but he lacks his own thoughts or personality. He simply follows the rabbi's orders. But that doesn't mean the Golem is harmless. If the rabbi forgets to take the tablet out from under the Golem's tongue, the creature may get into trouble. One forgotten Golem terrorized a village. He crashed through homes and shops. When the rabbi finally caught him and removed the tablet, the exhausted Golem crumbled into dust.

GOLEM TRIVIA

• This statue of the Golem (*above*) stands outside the
former Jewish section of the city of Prague in the Czech Republic.
• German filmmakers used the Golem story as the basis for a silent
movie. The film *The Golem* appeared in 1920.
• Golem is a Hebrew word meaning "shapeless mass" or "raw
material." The word refers to the monster being formed from clay.

In North America, many Native American groups tell tales of the Wendigo. According to the stories, Wendigo roams through forests and fields. He eats any hunters or other people he meets along the way. Wendigos are hard to fight because they are much bigger than ordinary humans. They are also covered with thick hair and have hearts made of ice. Some are missing their lips and toes. The only way to kill a Wendigo is to melt his icy heart.

The name *Wendigo* comes from the Ojibwa language. It means "evil spirit" or "evil spirit that devours mankind."

People have feared Wendigos and other bogeymen for centuries. But some bogeymen have more recent origins. For instance, from late 1966 to late 1967, people claimed to have seen a strange creature in the hills of West Virginia. They called him the Mothman. He stood well over six feet tall, with large wings and glowing red eyes. The Mothman didn't actually kill anyone, but he did frighten many locals with his sudden appearances. Skeptics, or nonbelievers, claimed the Mothman was just a large red owl or a very large crane. But no one could be sure. Adding to the mystery, on December 15, 1967, a bridge collapsed over the Ohio River on the West Virginia border. Forty-six people were killed in the disaster. Was the

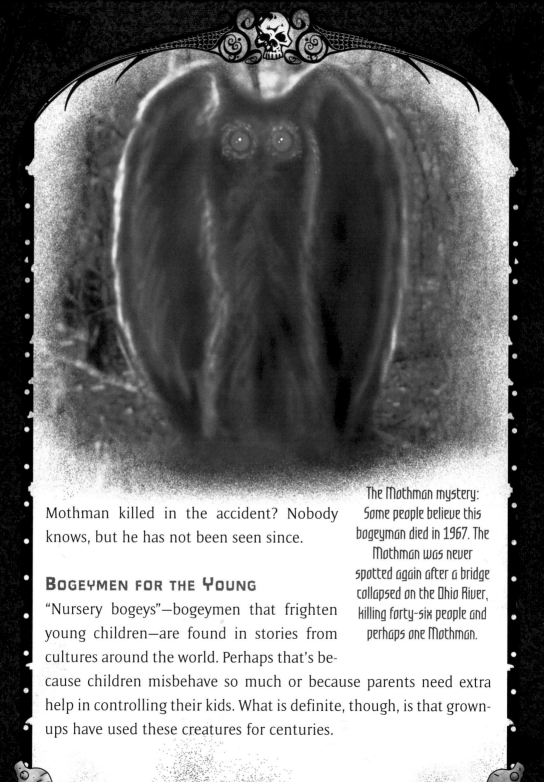

Mothman killed in the accident? Nobody knows, but he has not been seen since.

BOGEYMEN FOR THE YOUNG

"Nursery bogeys"—bogeymen that frighten young children—are found in stories from cultures around the world. Perhaps that's because children misbehave so much or because parents need extra help in controlling their kids. What is definite, though, is that grown-ups have used these creatures for centuries.

The Mothman mystery: Some people believe this bogeyman died in 1967. The Mothman was never spotted again after a bridge collapsed on the Ohio River, killing forty-six people and perhaps one Mothman.

Apparently, frightening children is a pretty big job. Great Britain alone has quite a few nursery bogeys. They include tales of Auld Scratty, Bug-a-boo, the Child Guzzler, Old Bloody Bones, and Raw Head. British children who steal fruit from trees may have to face Awd Goggie or Churnmilk Peg. Children who go into lakes or rivers without a parent's permission might find Jenny Greenteeth or Nellie Longarms waiting for them. The Boo-bagger carries around a huge bag for capturing young children. What does he do when he captures them? Most likely he eats them, since no children have ever escaped to say otherwise.

In North America, Native Americans have a long list of stories about nursery bogeys. Children of the Seneca Nation fear the Hagondes. He is sometimes called Long Nose because, well, he has a long nose. He is most famous for kidnapping and eating small children. The Apotamkin is a Native American nursery bogey from Maine. He is a hairy, human-like creature with big teeth and a big appetite. He is always ready to chew on children who misbehave.

A REAL-LIFE BOGEYMAN

Sometimes real people seem like bogeymen. Most commonly they are serial killers—murderers who kill many victims, one by one. Their acts of violence strike fear into the population. But legends of bogeymen rely on mystery to remain frightening. So whenever serial killers are captured, they are bogeymen no longer.

In London, England, in 1888, a mysterious killer roamed through the Whitechapel neighborhood. Five women there were found dead. Their throats had all been slashed. Some had their internal organs cut out.

The police thought that one man had done all the killings. In a letter to the London newspapers, a man claimed to be the killer. He called himself Jack the Ripper. The police thought Jack the Ripper might be a surgeon or a butcher, since he was clearly skilled with a knife. They suspected that he had committed a dozen other murders using similar methods. The police never found Jack, though. Whoever he was, he brought about far more fear than any made-up bogeyman. And his name has frightened people ever since.

This illustration of Jack the Ripper being caught red-handed appeared in an 1889 edition of the *Police News*. But the real-life murderer was never caught.

3 Bogeymen in Print

Some bogeymen have been with us for hundreds and thousands of years in myths and folktales. Others are more re-books. Writers have created bogeymen to raise the hair on our necks and send chills down our spines (usually at the same time). Of course, when bogeymen are safely contained on the printed page, they make us a little less nervous than they do when we think we see one in real life.

CASTS OF CHARACTERS

The earliest bogeyman in English literature is probably the creature Grendel. He appears in the Old English poem *Beowulf*, written in the A.D. 700s. In this story, Grendel has the nasty habit of crawling into the royal hall of the Danish king and attacking and eating people who sleep there. When the warrior Beowulf hears of this situation, he arrives with fourteen companions to fight Grendel. The men wait for the creature's arrival. Grendel shows up and eats one of Beowulf's friends right away. Then he seizes Beowulf. This turns out to be a big mistake. Beowulf wrestles mightily with Grendel and eventually tears out his arm. Bleeding heavily, Grendel retreats to his cave, where he dies. Later, Beowulf fights Grendel's mother, who

In 1971 the author John Gardner wrote a novel called *Grendel*. It tells the Beowulf story from the viewpoint of the monster (shown above).

wants to avenge her son's death. Beowulf kills her too. He might have bragged about these victories to his grandchildren. But he never gets the chance because a dragon kills him in battle. However, at least his name lives on.

In a story like *Beowulf,* it's easy to tell the bogeyman from the good guy. But *Dr. Jekyll and Mr. Hyde* (1886) is more confusing. This book by Robert Louis Stevenson tells the story of Dr. Henry Jekyll. Dr. Jekyll is convinced that people have two natures, one good and one evil.

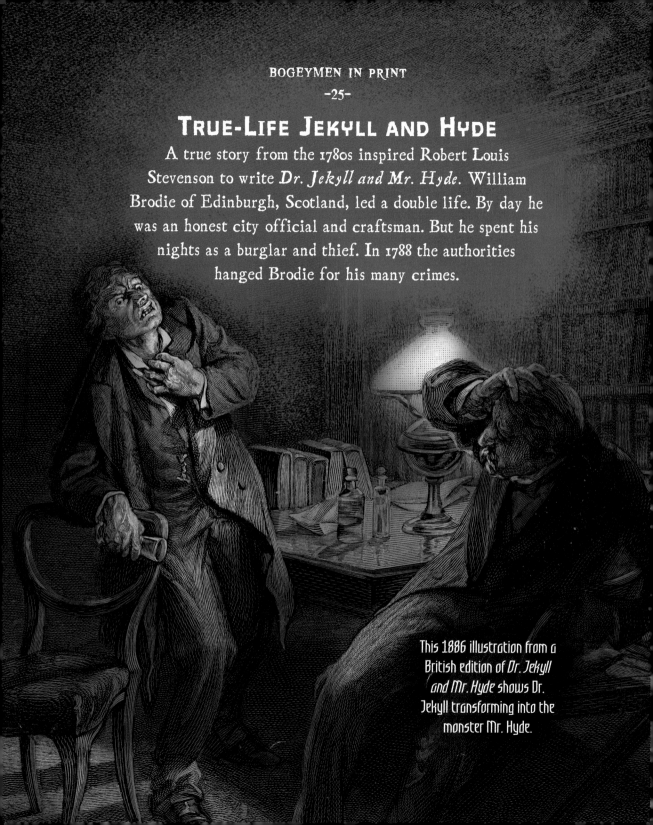

TRUE-LIFE JEKYLL AND HYDE

A true story from the 1780s inspired Robert Louis Stevenson to write *Dr. Jekyll and Mr. Hyde*. William Brodie of Edinburgh, Scotland, led a double life. By day he was an honest city official and craftsman. But he spent his nights as a burglar and thief. In 1788 the authorities hanged Brodie for his many crimes.

This 1886 illustration from a British edition of *Dr. Jekyll and Mr. Hyde* shows Dr. Jekyll transforming into the monster Mr. Hyde.

To test this theory, he experiments by taking a drug he has created. The drug transforms Dr. Jekyll into the evil Mr. Hyde. Hyde is small and hunched over. And while beauty may be only skin deep, Hyde's ugliness goes all the way down to his soul. He prowls the city, committing crimes against innocent residents. Hyde eventually returns to his Jekyll form, but the story doesn't end there. Dr. Jekyll discovers that the drug's effects are unpredictable. He worries that Mr. Hyde might take control of him permanently. To keep that from happening, Dr. Jekyll kills himself. The tragedy is made greater by the larger idea that we may all have a bogeyman hidden inside us.

Harper Lee's famous novel *To Kill a Mockingbird* (1960) features a bogeyman

Robert Duvall played bogeyman Boo Radley in the 1962 film version of *To Kill a Mockingbird*, along with Mary Badham as Scout. Boo turned out to be not so scary after all. Boo's kindness is a rarity among bogeymen.

named Boo Radley—at least that's what the townspeople think. They avoid him as much as possible. They say he leaves his house only at night, to hunt squirrels and cats. But three children—Jem, Scout, and Dill—become curious about Boo. They discover that while Boo is certainly a damaged human being, he also has a kindly nature. Later, Boo saves their lives and turns out to be a hero.

THRILLS, CHILLS, AND SOME UNEXPECTED LAUGHS

Horror writer Stephen King specializes in supernatural creatures. He has written about bogeymen more than once. The first piece was a short story called "The Boogeyman" (1978). The tale features a man who visits a psychiatrist. The man claims that a bogeyman hides in his bedroom closets. More disturbingly, the man claims that the creature has killed his three children. Is the man telling the truth—or is he simply pretending to be crazy?

Novelist Stephen King has used his home state of Maine as the locale for many of his books, including *It*.

A novel by King, *It* (1986), concerns seven friends and a bogeyman. The seven friends get together after a long time apart. The reunion takes place in their

childhood home of Derry, Maine. Twenty-eight years earlier, as teenagers, the seven had fought an evil creature called It that had terrorized the town's children. Although the teenagers had defeated the creature, It was not necessarily gone forever. The teenagers had made a solemn promise to one another: if It ever reappeared, they would come home to fight again. And that time has come.

It might seem difficult for bogeymen to be scary and funny at the same time. But a few of them have managed to do so. One is Fungus, the main character in *Fungus the Bogeyman* by Raymond Briggs (1979). This cartoon-style novel for children concerns an ordinary bogeyman whose job is to scare human beings. But none of what Fungus does—knocking over garbage cans, waking sleeping babies—is too scary. Fungus lives underground in a bogeyman world with his wife and children. Their home smells disgusting and looks worse, which is just the way they like it. The best parts of the book are all the great details of Fungus's everyday life as a bogeyman.

In the classic comic strip *Calvin and Hobbes* (1985–1995), young Calvin often encounters bogeymen. They lie under his bed and lurk in his closet. Whatever they are, Calvin knows they are out to get him.

This *Calvin and Hobbes* comic strip ran originally in August 1992. Like many Calvin comics, it features Calvin being scared by the bogeymen he thinks are under his bed.

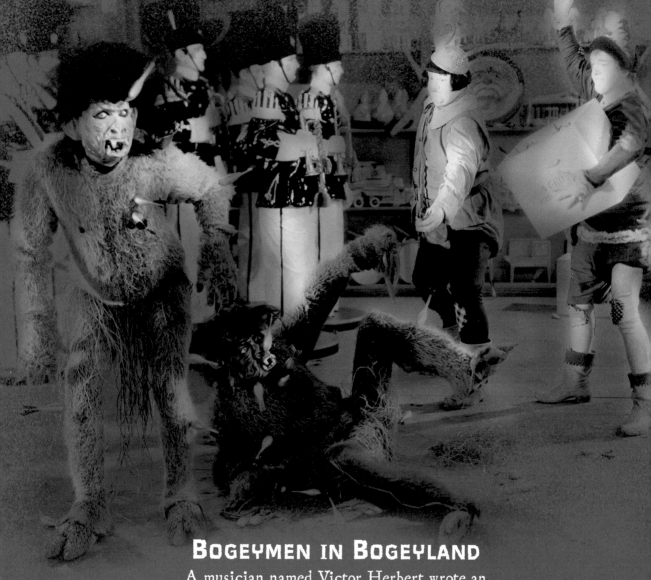

BOGEYMEN IN BOGEYLAND
A musician named Victor Herbert wrote an
operetta (a comic opera) called *Babes in Toyland* in 1903.
In this story, bogeymen live in a place called Bogeyland. It lies just
across a river from a much nicer place called Toyland.
The river that separates the two places is filled with crocodiles.
In this 1934 movie version of *Babes in Toyland*, Stan Laurel
and Oliver Hardy *(above)* play the lead bogeymen roles.

And he knows they will show no mercy if they do. To escape their clutches, Calvin must depend on his own smarts. He doesn't get any help from his partner, the tiger Hobbes, who doesn't believe in bogeymen.

You don't often hear a bogeyman complain about his reputation. But that's just what happens in *Psssst! It's Me . . . the Bogeyman* (1998) by Barbara Park. In this book for young readers, an under-the-bed bogeyman complains to a boy on the bed above him. The bogeyman is upset about a fraud—a fake bogeyman who's grabbing newspaper headlines. It's not right, he complains, that the fake bogeyman does not follow the rules of the "Official Bogeyman Contract." For the boy, a whiny bogeyman is not as frightening as an evil one. But the bogeyman still presents challenges.

The His Dark Materials series of books by Philip Pullman *(above)* includes *The Subtle Knife*, which features bogeymen called Spectres. A movie based on the first book in the series, *The Golden Compass*, was released in 2007. It stars Nicole Kidman and Daniel Craig.

Philip Pullman's book *The Subtle Knife* (1997) takes bogeymen to another world. In this strange landscape, the bogeymen are invisible creatures

called Spectres. They are no mere ghosts. They are real bogeymen who harm older children and adults. A Spectre reveals itself to a victim as a shimmering in the air. Such shimmerings should be avoided at all costs, because when a Spectre catches a victim, it sucks out his or her soul, leaving behind an empty shell of a body. And it doesn't help that humans cannot kill Spectres. Most people, having to choose between facing a Spectre or simply dying, would pick death every time.

Philip Pullman's *The Subtle Knife* is the second part of a trilogy (three-part series) called His Dark Materials. The series begins with *The Golden Compass* (1995) and ends with *The Amber Spyglass* (2000).

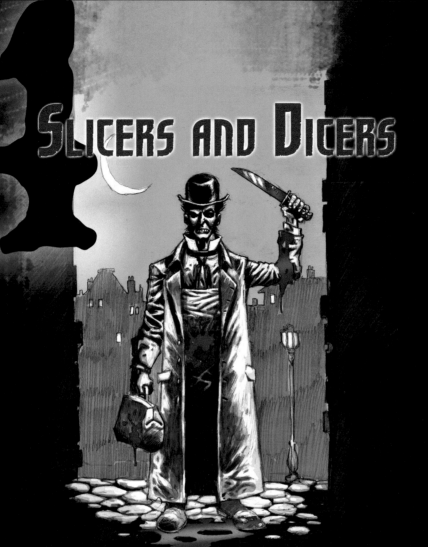

Slicers and Dicers

Reading about bogeymen can be scary enough. But seeing them in movies can really make you jump. Unlike, say, vampires or werewolves, bogeymen don't always scare people automatically, just by showing up on screen. They have to work a little harder to inspire fear and terror. And unlike many monsters, they usually lack supernatural powers. So to get under your skin, they have to carve out their own distinctive image.

THE RIPPER ON SCREEN

The real-life story of Jack the Ripper has been made into many films. Jack the Ripper movies began in the silent-movie era, when nobody could hear you scream—at least not on film. The great director Alfred

A 1944 remake of *The Lodger* featured U.S. actor Laird Cregar as the suspected bogeyman renting a room from a couple in London.

Hitchcock first gained attention for a silent film called *The Lodger* (1927), which was partly inspired by the Jack the Ripper legend. The story concerns a couple in London. They believe that the man renting a room from them is an evil killer who has been terrorizing the city. Is he or isn't he? That's the question. The film was remade in the 1930s and 1940s, each time with increasingly frightening scenes.

In 1979 two movies featured Jack the Ripper. In *Time After Time,* Malcolm McDowell plays the real-life British author H. G. Wells. Wells follows Jack the Ripper across time and space to modern-day San Francisco, California. There, Wells hopes to stop Jack from killing again. In *Murder by Decree,* fiction and real life again overlap as the fictional detective Sherlock Holmes (played by Christopher Plummer) investigates the real-life Whitechapel murders.

The animated movie *Monsters, Inc.* (2001) explained that monsters that appear from the closet or under the bed come from another dimension, where all kinds of monsters live.

TEENAGERS IN TROUBLE

In the late 1970s and early 1980s, horror movies really heated up. A few of the most famous movie bogeymen came to life during this period. The fictional Michael Myers (played mostly by stuntmen) was one of them. In *Halloween* (1978), Michael starts out as an ordinary boy. He doesn't seem like a bogeyman—at least not at first. But the situation changes when, at the age of six, he kills his teenage sister with a kitchen knife. The authorities lock up Michael in a hospital. A doctor cares for him for the next fifteen years. The doctor is convinced that Michael is evil. Things might have been okay if Michael had remained locked up. But when he escapes and begins to kill again (perhaps trying to make up for lost time), people are right to be afraid.

In the movies, it's never a good sign when a boy drowns at summer camp. It's an even worse sign when two camp counselors are murdered the next year. Both of these bad signs show up in *Friday the 13th*

Jason Voorhees is a murderous bogeyman in the Friday the 13th movies.

(1980). In the many Friday the 13th movies that followed, the drowned boy, Jason Voorhees (also played by stuntmen), has grown up to become a bogeyman. He wears a hockey mask and carries a large knife called a machete. Jason doesn't do much talking. He only mumbles and groans, letting his machete speak for him. Sadly for his many victims, his machete has a number of points to make.

Freddy Krueger is one of the scariest, evilest bogeymen on film. He doesn't attack in a real place, such as a dark alley, where at least a victim has a chance to get away. He attacks people in their dreams. In *A Nightmare on Elm Street* (1984), a teenage girl named Nancy has nightmares about a strange man named Freddy Krueger.

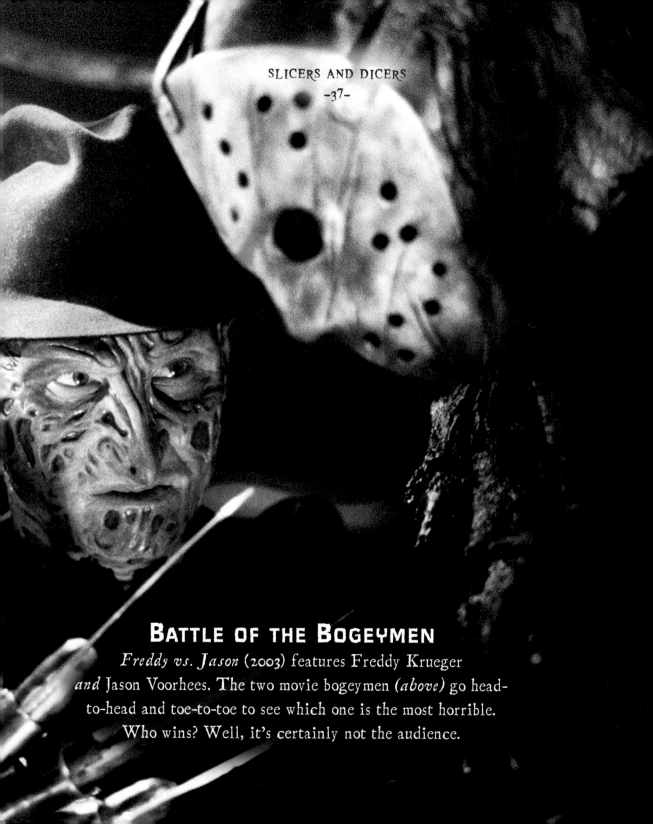

BATTLE OF THE BOGEYMEN

Freddy vs. Jason (2003) features Freddy Krueger
and Jason Voorhees. The two movie bogeymen (*above*) go head-
to-head and toe-to-toe to see which one is the most horrible.
Who wins? Well, it's certainly not the audience.

Actor Robert Englund has played bogeyman Freddy Krueger in all the Nightmare on Elm Street movies, starting in 1984.

He is burned and scarred and wears a razor-fingered glove on one hand. Nancy discovers that her friends are having nightmares about the same man. Then one of her friends turns up dead. Nancy discovers that if Freddy kills you in your dream, you will also die in real life. Knowing that Freddy is after her, she must race against time, staying awake long enough to defeat him. Of course, for the moviemakers, it made more sense (and more money) to keep Freddy alive. That way, they could make sequels (movies that continue to use the same characters). So Freddy is never truly destroyed. In each of the next six Nightmare movies, Freddy Krueger continues to show his dark side (the only one he has).

LAUGH TILL YOU SCREAM

Many bogeyman movies of the 1970s and 1980s followed a similar pattern. The victims were usually teenagers, especially teenage girls. The bogeymen were haunted souls, disturbed by some great tragedy. In the 1990s, moviemakers started adding a new twist to bogeyman movies—humor. The new movies made fun of the earlier, typical bogeyman movies. But they were still scary.

In *Scream* (1996), a mysterious killer threatens a teenage girl named Sidney Prescott (played by Neve Campbell). To make matters worse, this killer calls his victims ahead of time to taunt them. *Scream* and its sequels breathed new life into horror films by mocking horror movies while still scaring viewers' pants off.

The bogeyman scares Sidney Prescott over the phone, before coming after her. Neve Campbell played Prescott in all three Scream movies.

The Scary Movie series (2000–2006) also pokes fun at earlier horror films. This series features a young woman named Cindy Campbell. Along with her friends, she is menaced by a mysterious bad guy (as if

The headline on the poster for *Scary Movie* was "No mercy. No shame. No sequel." But the movie's success led to *Scary Movie 2*. The poster for that movie read, "We lied."

teenage girls don't have enough problems already). The first film in the series, *Scary Movie,* made jokes about several earlier scary movies, including *The Sixth Sense* and *I Know What You Did Last Summer.* There have been four Scary Movies in all. Each has made fun of other films and bogeymen in general.

BOGEYMEN IN SPACE

It seems that no place is safe from bogeymen—not even outer space. *Serenity* (2005) follows a group of outer-space adventurers. They must dodge the authorities as well as bogeymen known as the Reavers. The Reavers travel through the galaxy, fighting, torturing, murdering, and feasting on other species as they go. When a spaceship encounters the Reavers, it's not a question of whether to stay and fight. The question is: how fast can the space travelers run away?

The outer-space adventurers in *Serenity* keep an eye out for bogeymen called Reavers. The movie *Serenity* was a continuation of the TV show *Firefly,* which also featured Reavers.

Running away is actually a pretty good tactic when you're facing any kind of bogeyman. Sure, you may stand a chance of defeating him, especially if you're very lucky. But the odds are not in your favor. An old saying tells us that the person "who fights and runs away lives to fight another day." When dealing with bogeymen, it would be wise to keep that saying in mind.

MORE BOGEYMEN FROM AROUND THE WORLD

Babaroga (Serbia and Croatia): Babaroga, or Old Woman, will kidnap and eat children who misbehave. She's a lot like Baba Yaga, the famous Russian witch.

Babay (Russia): The Babay is an old man with a bag for collecting unruly children. He usually hides under the bed.

Bicho Papão (Brazil): This bogeyman is part human, part animal. His name means "eating beast," and he eats up children who misbehave.

Bonhomme Sept-Heures (Quebec, Canada): This bogeyman, whose name means "Mister Seven O'Clock," visits houses around seven at night. If children won't go to bed, he takes them back to his cave and eats them.

Bussemand (Denmark): The Danish bogeyman hides under the bed and grabs children who won't go to sleep at bedtime.

Cucuy (Mexico): This Mexican bogeyman is a small creature with glowing red eyes. It hides in closets and under beds.

Emmo-o (Japan): In the Japanese Buddhist tradition, Emmo-o is the god of the underworld. He does double duty as a bogeyman, scaring children who misbehave.

Hombre del Saco (Latin America): the Hombre del Saco, or Bag Man, looks like a hobo. He carries a sack for gathering up children who disobey.

L'uomo Nero (Italy): The Italian bogeyman is a tall man dressed in a heavy black coat. A black hood hides his face. His name means "the black man."

Shellycoat (Scotland): This bogeyman haunts rivers and streams. He wears a coat of shells, which explains his name.

Shurale (Russia): According to Russian folklore, this bogeyman haunts the forests at night.

Source Notes

11 Eliza Gutch and Mabel Peacock, *County Folk-Lore, vol. 5, Examples of Printed Folk-Lore Concerning Lincolnshire* (London: Folk-Lore Society, 1908), 383–384.

Selected Bibliography

Briggs, Katharine. *An Encyclopedia of Fairies, Hobgoblins, Brownies, Bogies and Other Supernatural Creatures.* New York: Pantheon Books, 1976.

Guiley, Rosemary Ellen. *The Encyclopedia of Vampires, Werewolves and Other Monsters.* New York: Checkmark Books, 2005.

Keel, John A. *The Complete Guide to Mysterious Beings.* New York: Doubleday, 1994.

Keightley, Thomas. *The World Guide to Gnomes, Fairies, Elves and Other Little People.* New York: Gramercy Books, 2000.

Rose, Carol. *Giants, Monsters & Dragons: An Encyclopedia of Folklore, Legend, and Myth.* New York: W. W. Norton and Company, 2000.

Further Reading and Websites

Briggs, Raymond. *Fungus the Bogeyman.* New York: Random House, 1979. This comic-book-style novel investigates the underground world of "Bogeydom," especially the bogeyman Fungus and his family.

Cooper, Susan. *The Boggart.* New York: Atheneum, 1993. When the Volnick family returns home from Scotland, young Emily and Jessup find that a mischievous Boggart has accidentally returned with them. Getting the Boggart back home is not easily accomplished. It requires an inspired mix of ancient folklore and modern technology.

Encyclopedia Mythica

http://www.pantheon.org/

This website is devoted to all kinds of myths and mythical creatures. Visitors can find articles on bogeymen from around the world.

Herbst, Judith. *Monsters*. Minneapolis: Lerner Publications Company, 2005. Herbst recounts the legends and examines the myths surrounding several monsters, including the Mothman.

King, Stephen. *It*. New York: Viking, 1986. Twenty-eight years earlier, seven Maine teenagers successfully battled an evil creature in their hometown. They promised one another that if the creature ever returned, they would come home to fight again. And that moment has come.

Lee, Harper. *To Kill a Mockingbird*. New York: Lippincott, 1960. This award-winning novel, set in Alabama during the 1930s, follows three years in the life of Scout Finch, who is eight when the story begins. The book examines views about the local bogeyman, Boo Radley, and larger issues of race surrounding a sensational rape trial.

Pullman, Philip. *The Subtle Knife*. New York: Alfred A. Knopf, 1997. This book is the middle volume in the His Dark Materials trilogy. The story follows Will Parry as he travels from our world to another. Before leaving he meets Lyra Belacqua, whose destiny and adventures become entangled with his own.

Stevenson, Robert Louis. *Dr. Jekyll and Mr. Hyde*. 1886. Reprint, New York: Pocket Books, 1972. A well-meaning nineteenth-century doctor experiments on himself. The experiment unleashes the dark side of his personality and body. This changeover threatens his mind and his soul.

MOVIES

Murder by Decree. DVD. Troy, MI: Anchor Bay Entertainment, 2003. In this movie from 1979, Sherlock Holmes pursues one of the most famous real-life bogeymen, Jack the Ripper.

Serenity. DVD. Universal City, CA: Universal Studios, 2005. A ragtag band of smugglers tries to avoid both an evil space empire and interstellar bogeymen.

Time After Time. DVD. Burbank, CA: Warner Home Video, 2002. The British author H. G. Wells follows the infamous Jack the Ripper through time into modern-day San Francisco. There, Wells tries to keep Jack from starting another killing spree.

To Kill a Mockingbird. DVD. Universal City, CA: Universal Studios, 2005. This screen adaptation of Harper Lee's award-winning novel remains a classic of American cinema, and tells the story of Atticus Finch and his children, Scout and Jem, who discover that the bogeyman next door, Boo Radley, isn't so scary. Boo turns out to be a hero in the end.

INDEX

ABOUT THE AUTHOR

Stephen Krensky is the author of many fiction and nonfiction books for children, including titles in the On My Own Folklore series and *Bigfoot*, *The Bogeyman*, *Dragons*, *Frankenstein*, *Ghosts*, *The Mummy*, *Vampires*, *Watchers in the Woods*, *Werewolves*, and *Zombies*. When he isn't hunched over his computer, he makes school visits and teaches writing workshops. In his free time, he enjoys playing tennis and softball and reading books by other people. Krensky lives in Massachusetts with his wife, Joan, and their family.

PHOTO ACKNOWLEDGMENTS

The photographs in this book are used with the permission of: Courtesy of Paramount Pictures. FRIDAY THE 13th PART VII: THE NEW BLOOD © Paramount Pictures. All Rights Reserved. Photo provided by © Photofest, p. 2-3; © Hulton Archive/Getty Images, pp. 9, 11, 21; © North Wind Picture Archives, p. 10; © Mary Evans Picture Library/The Image Works, p. 13; © Frank Scherschel/Time Life Pictures/Getty Images, p. 17; © William M. Rebsamen/Fortean Picture Library, p. 19; © The British Library/HIP/The Image Works, p. 24; © Kean Collection/Hulton Archive/Getty Images, p. 25; Courtesy of Universal Studios Licensing LLLP. Photo provided by © Photofest, pp. 26, 41; © Kevin Winter/Getty Images Entertainment/Getty Images, p. 27; CALVIN AND HOBBES © 1992 Watterson. Dist. By UNIVERSAL PRESS SYNDICATE. Reprint with Permission. All rights reserved, p. 28; © MGM/Photofest, p. 29; © MJ Kim/Getty Images Entertainment/Getty Images, p. 30; "THE LODGER" © 1944 Twentieth Century Fox. All rights reserved. Photo provided by © Hulton Archive/Getty Images, p. 34; Courtesy of Paramount Pictures. FRIDAY THE 13th PART VII: THE NEW BLOOD © Paramount Pictures. All Rights Reserved. Photo provided by © Photofest, p. 36; "Freddy vs. Jason" © MMIII, New Line Productions, Inc. All rights reserved. Photo by James Dittiger. Photo appears courtesy of New Line Productions, Inc., p. 37; "A Nightmare on Elm Street" © MCMLXXXIV, New Line Productions, Inc. All rights reserved. Photo by James Dittiger. Photo appears courtesy of New Line Productions, Inc., p. 38; Photo by David Moir/Courtesy of Miramax Film Corp., p. 39; Photo by Chris Large/Courtesy of Miramax Film Corp., p. 40. Illustrations © Bill Hauser/Independent Picture Service, pp. 1, 6, 14-15, 22-23, 32, 42. All page background illustrations © Bill Hauser/Independent Picture Service. Front cover: "Freddy vs. Jason" © MMIII, New Line Productions, Inc. All rights reserved. Photo by James Dittiger. Photo appears courtesy of New Line Productions, Inc.